Light Cooking ™

QUICK & EASY
MEALS IN 30 MINUTES

Healthy, Low Fat and Delicious!

PUBLICATIONS INTERNATIONAL, LTD.

Light Cooking is a trademark of Publications International, Ltd.

Food Guide Pyramid source: U.S. Department of Agriculture/U.S. Department of Health and Human Services.

Recipe Development: Mary Holloway, Food Consultant
Nutritional Analysis: Linda R. Yoakam, M.S., R.D.

Photography: Burke/Triolo Productions, Culver City, CA

Pictured on the front cover: Glazed Stuffed Pork Chops *(page 30).*
Pictured on the inside front cover: Spicy Pork Stir-Fry *(page 26).*
Pictured on the inside back cover: Mandarin Chicken Salad *(page 50).*
Pictured on the back cover *(clockwise from top left):* Hummus Pita Sandwiches *(page 88),* Pasta Primavera with Ricotta and Herbs *(page 78),* Chicken Breasts with Crabmeat Stuffing *(page 40)* and Stir-Fry Shrimp and Snow Peas *(page 60).*

ISBN: 0-7853-1117-3

Manufactured in U.S.A.

8   7   6   5   4   3   2   1

Microwave Cooking: Microwave ovens vary in wattage. The microwave cooking times given in this publication are approximate. Use the cooking times as guidelines and check for doneness before adding more time. Consult manufacturer's instructions for suitable microwave-safe cooking dishes.

CONTENTS

LESSONS IN SMART EATING

Today, people everywhere are more aware than ever before about the importance of maintaining a healthful lifestyle. In addition to proper exercise, this includes eating foods that are lower in fat, sodium and cholesterol. The goal of *Light Cooking* is to provide today's cook with easy-to-prepare recipes that taste great, yet easily fit into your dietary goals. Eating well is a matter of making smarter choices about the foods you eat. Preparing the recipes in *Light Cooking* is your first step toward making smart choices a delicious reality.

A Balanced Diet

The U.S. Department of Agriculture and the Department of Health and Human Services have developed a Food Guide Pyramid to illustrate how easy it is to eat a healthier diet. It is not a rigid prescription, but rather a general guide that lets you choose a healthful diet that's right for you. It calls for eating a wide variety of foods to get the nutrients you need and, at the same time, the right amount of calories to maintain a healthy weight.

Food Guide Pyramid
A Guide to Daily Food Choices

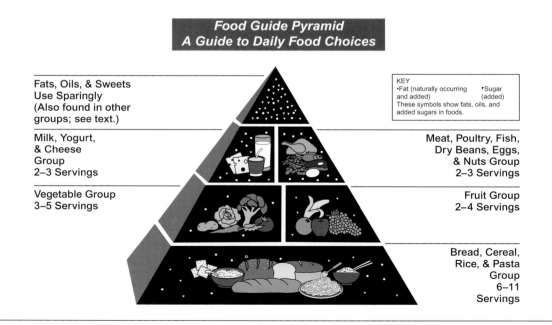

Fats, Oils, & Sweets
Use Sparingly
(Also found in other
groups; see text.)

KEY
•Fat (naturally occurring   ▼Sugar
and added)   (added)
These symbols show fats, oils, and
added sugars in foods.

Milk, Yogurt,
& Cheese
Group
2–3 Servings

Meat, Poultry, Fish,
Dry Beans, Eggs,
& Nuts Group
2–3 Servings

Vegetable Group
3–5 Servings

Fruit Group
2–4 Servings

Bread, Cereal,
Rice, & Pasta
Group
6–11
Servings

The number of servings, and consequently, the number of calories a person can eat each day, is determined by a number of factors, including age, weight, height, activity level and gender. Sedentary women and some older adults need about 1,600 calories each day. For most children, teenage girls, active women and many sedentary men, 2,000 calories is about right. Teenage boys, active men and some very active women use about 2,800 calories each day. Use the chart below to determine how many servings you need for your calorie level.

Personalized Food Group Servings for Different Calorie Levels*			
	1,600	2,000	2,800
Bread Group Servings	6	8	11
Vegetable Group Servings	3	4	5
Fruit Group Servings	2	3	4
Milk Group Servings	2–3**	2–3**	2–3**
Meat Group Servings (ounces)	5	6	7

* Numbers may be rounded.
** Women who are pregnant or breast-feeding, teenagers and young adults to age 24 need 3 or more servings.

Lower Fat for Healthier Living

It is widely known that most Americans' diets are too high in fat. A low fat diet reduces your risk of getting certain diseases and helps you maintain a healthy weight. Studies have shown that eating more than the recommended amount of fat (especially saturated fat) is associated with increased blood cholesterol levels in some adults. A high blood cholesterol level is associated with increased risk for heart disease. A high fat diet may also increase your chances for obesity and some types of cancer.

Nutrition experts recommend diets that contain 30% or less of total daily calories from fat. The "30% calories from fat" goal applies to a total diet over time, not to a single food, serving of a recipe or meal. To find the approximate percentage of calories from fat use this easy 3-step process:

1 Multiply the grams of fat per serving by 9 (there are 9 calories in each gram of fat), to give you the number of calories from fat per serving.

2 Divide by the total number of calories per serving.

3 Multiply by 100%.

For example, imagine a 200 calorie sandwich that has 10 grams of fat.
To find the percentage of calories from fat, first multiply the grams of fat by 9:

$10 \times 9 = 90$

Then, divide by the total number of calories in a serving:

$90 \div 200 = .45$

Multiply by 100% to get the percentage of calories from fat:

$.45 \times 100\% = 45\%$

You may find doing all this math tiresome, so an easier way to keep track of the fat in your diet is to calculate the total *grams* of fat appropriate to your caloric intake, then keep a running count of fat grams over the course of a day. The Nutrition Reference Chart on page 92 lists recommended daily fat intakes based on calorie level.

Defining "Fat Free"

It is important to take the time to read food labels carefully. For example, you'll find many food products on the grocery store shelves making claims such as "97% fat free." This does not necessarily mean that 97% of the *calories* are free from fat (or that only 3 percent of calories come from fat). Often these numbers are calculated by weight. This means that out of 100 grams of this food, 3 grams are fat. Depending on what else is in the food, the percentage of calories from fat can be quite high. You may find that the percent of calories *from fat* can be as high as 50%.

Daily Values

Fat has become the focus of many diets and eating plans. This is because most Americans' diets are too high in fat. However, there are other important nutrients to be aware of, including saturated fat, sodium, cholesterol, protein, carbohydrates and several vitamins and minerals. Daily values for these nutrients have been established by the government and reflect current nutritional recommendations for a 2,000 calorie reference diet. They are appropriate for most adults and children (age 4 or older) and provide excellent guidelines for an overall healthy diet. The chart on page 92 gives the daily values for 11 different items.

Nutritional Analysis

Every recipe in *Light Cooking* is followed by a nutritional analysis block that lists certain nutrient values for a single serving.

■ The analysis of each recipe includes all the ingredients that are listed in that recipe, *except* ingredients labeled as "optional" or "for garnish."

■ If a range is given in the yield of a recipe ("Makes 6 to 8 servings" for example), the *lower* yield was used to calculate the per serving information.

■ If a range is offered for an ingredient ("¼ to ⅛ teaspoon" for example), the *first* amount given was used to calculate the nutrition information.

■ If an ingredient is presented with an option ("2 cups hot cooked rice or noodles" for example), the *first* item listed was used to calculate the nutritional information.

■ Foods shown in photographs on the same serving plate and offered as "serve with" suggestions at the end of a recipe are *not* included in the recipe analysis unless they are listed in the ingredient list.

■ Meat should be trimmed of all visible fat since this is reflected in the nutritional analysis.

■ In recipes calling for cooked rice or noodles, the analysis was based on rice or noodles that were prepared without added salt or fat unless otherwise mentioned in the recipe.

The nutrition information that appears with each recipe was calculated by an independent nutrition consulting firm. Every effort has been made to check the accuracy of these numbers. However, because numerous variables account for a wide range of values in certain foods, all analyses that appear in this book should be considered approximate.

The recipes in this publication are *not* intended as a medically therapeutic program, nor as a substitute for medically approved diet plans for people on fat, cholesterol or sodium restricted diets. You should consult your physician before beginning any diet plan. The recipes offered here can be a part of a healthy lifestyle that meets recognized dietary guidelines. A healthy lifestyle includes not only eating a balanced diet, but engaging in proper exercise as well.

All the ingredients called for in these recipes are generally available in large supermarkets, so there is no need to go to specialty or health food stores. You'll also see an ever-increasing amount of reduced fat and nonfat products available in local markets. Take advantage of these items to reduce your daily fat intake even more.

Cooking Healthier

When cooking great-tasting low fat meals, you will find some techniques or ingredients are different from traditional cooking. Fat serves as a flavor enhancer and gives foods a distinctive and desirable texture. In order to compensate for the lack of fat and still give great-tasting results, many of the *Light Cooking* recipes call for a selection of herbs or a combination of fresh vegetables. A wide variety of grains and pastas are also used. Many of the recipes call for alternative protein sources, such as dried beans or tofu. Often meat is included in a recipe as an accent flavor rather than the star attraction. Vegetables are often "sautéed" in a small amount of broth rather than oil. Applesauce may be added to baked goods to give a texture similar to full fat foods. These are all simple changes that you can easily make when you start cooking healthy!

Meals in 30 Minutes

If your lifestyle is anything like most of today's families, you don't have a lot of time for cooking healthful meals. *Light Cooking Quick & Easy Meals in 30 Minutes* is the perfect solution. It is filled with easy-to-prepare recipes that are low in fat, cholesterol and sodium—and best of all, these recipes take 30 minutes or less to prepare. Many are entrées that require no other accompaniment. Others need only hot bread, a steamed vegetable or fresh fruit to round out the meal.

To guide you in meal planning, each recipe includes a "ready to serve" time. These are based on the approximate amount of time needed to assemble and prepare ingredients prior to cooking and the minimum amount of time required to cook, broil, microwave or chill the foods in the recipes. In addition, these recipes have been developed for the most efficient use of your time. Some preparation steps, such as chopping, slicing and shredding are completed before cooking begins. Other preparation steps are done during cooking (i.e., vegetables are chopped while waiting for water to boil, etc.).

Helpful Hints

■ Plan at least some of a week's meals in advance. This helps to keep shopping trips to a minimum, to ensure timely defrosting and to allow for sufficient marinating time.

■ Plan to use leftovers. For instance, roast a chicken or buy a rotisserie chicken from the supermarket and plan to use the leftovers in a recipe that requires cooked chicken.

■ Read recipes thoroughly before making a grocery list so no ingredients are forgotten. Keep a grocery list in a convenient location and add items as you or family members think of them.

■ Take advantage of the many nutritious convenience items now available in supermarkets. Purchase cut-up raw vegetables from the produce section or salad bar. Choose from a wide range of packaged salad mixes that eliminate all at-home preparation; some contain a variety of baby lettuces and others combine lettuce with carrots, cabbage and other vegetables. Presliced fruits from the supermarket salad bar speed preparation of fruit salads. They can also be used for healthful no-fuss desserts. Cheeses that have been shredded, boneless skinless chicken breasts and marinated meats and poultry are other examples of the wealth of time savers you will find at the supermarket.

■ Prepare double batches of soups, spaghetti sauces and casseroles and freeze half for later use. On weekends when you have more time, prepare two different dishes and serve one the next day.

■ Enlist your family to help with meal preparation and cleanup.

■ Complete meals with simple accompaniments, such as bakery breads, steamed or raw vegetables or fresh fruit—all healthful busy-day choices.

BEEF

ROAST BEEF AND PASTA SALAD

This easy-to-make salad is
brimming with color, flavor
and fiber. To cut preparation
time to under 10 minutes,
use leftover pasta.

9 ounces uncooked radiatore pasta
6 ounces lean roast beef
1 can (15 ounces) kidney beans, drained and rinsed
1 can (15 ounces) whole baby corn, drained and rinsed
1 can (10 ounces) diced tomatoes and green chilies
1 cup cherry tomato halves
2 tablespoons minced fresh parsley
1 tablespoon minced fresh oregano
¼ cup olive oil
½ cup sliced ripe olives (optional)

1 Cook radiatore according to package directions, omitting salt; drain. Rinse with cold water; drain.

2 Slice beef into thin strips. Combine pasta, beef and remaining ingredients in large bowl. Toss to coat. Garnish with fresh oregano, if desired.   *Makes 6 servings*

Ready to serve in 25 minutes.

Nutrients per Serving:

Calories	411
(26% of calories from fat)	
Total Fat	13 g
Saturated Fat	2 g
Cholesterol	23 mg
Sodium	576 mg
Carbohydrate	58 g
Dietary Fiber	8 g
Protein	22 g
Calcium	29 mg
Iron	3 mg
Vitamin A	68 RE
Vitamin C	17 mg

DIETARY EXCHANGES:
3 Starch/Bread, 2 Lean
Meat, 1 Vegetable, 1½ Fat

KANSAS CITY STEAK SOUP

*Despite its name, this filling
vegetable-beef soup has
traditionally been made
with ground beef. In this
updated version, the
percentage of calories from
fat has been pared to 23%,
but the full, rich flavor
remains. If time permits,
allow the soup to simmer an
additional 30 minutes—the
flavors just get better
and better.*

Nonstick cooking spray
½ pound ground sirloin or ground round beef
1 cup chopped onion
3 cups frozen mixed vegetables
1 cup sliced celery
1 can (14½ ounces) stewed tomatoes, undrained
1 beef bouillon cube
½ to 1 teaspoon ground black pepper
2 cups water
½ cup all-purpose flour
1 can (10½ ounces) defatted beef broth

1 Spray Dutch oven with cooking spray. Heat over medium-high heat until hot. Add beef and onion. Cook and stir 5 minutes or until beef is browned.

2 Add mixed vegetables, celery, tomatoes and juice, bouillon cube, pepper and water. Bring to a boil. Whisk together flour and beef broth until smooth; add to beef mixture, stirring constantly. Return mixture to a boil. Reduce heat to low. Cover and simmer 15 minutes, stirring frequently. *Makes 6 servings*

Ready to serve in 30 minutes.

Nutrients per Serving:

Calories	198
(23% of calories from fat)	
Total Fat	5 g
Saturated Fat	2 g
Cholesterol	23 mg
Sodium	598 mg
Carbohydrate	27 g
Dietary Fiber	5 g
Protein	13 g
Calcium	63 mg
Iron	3 mg
Vitamin A	428 RE
Vitamin C	15 mg

DIETARY EXCHANGES:
½ Starch/Bread, 1 Lean
Meat, 3½ Vegetable, ½ Fat

BEEF STROGANOFF AND ZUCCHINI TOPPED POTATOES

❖

*This fabulous and filling
recipe is perfect for those
who love meat and potatoes.
The percent of calories from
fat is a respectable 25%. To
lower fat even more, use
nonfat sour cream.*

❖

Nutrients per Serving:

Calories	451
(25% of calories from fat)	
Total Fat	13 g
Saturated Fat	4 g
Cholesterol	62 mg
Sodium	406 mg
Carbohydrate	62 g
Dietary Fiber	1 g
Protein	23 g
Calcium	71 mg
Iron	3 mg
Vitamin A	28 RE
Vitamin C	44 mg

DIETARY EXCHANGES:
3½ Starch/Bread, 2½ Lean
Meat, 1 Vegetable, 1 Fat

4 large baking potatoes (8 ounces each)
¾ pound ground round beef
¾ cup chopped onion
1 cup sliced mushrooms
1 beef bouillon cube
2 tablespoons ketchup
1 teaspoon Worcestershire sauce
¼ teaspoon ground black pepper
¼ teaspoon hot pepper sauce
1 medium zucchini, cut into julienned strips
½ cup low fat sour cream, divided

1 Pierce potatoes in several places with fork. Place in microwave oven on paper towel. Microwave potatoes at HIGH 15 minutes or until softened. Wrap in paper towels; let stand 5 minutes.

2 Heat large nonstick skillet over medium-high heat until hot. Add beef and onion. Cook and stir 5 minutes or until beef is browned. Add all remaining ingredients except zucchini and sour cream. Cover and simmer 5 minutes. Add zucchini. Cover and cook 3 minutes. Remove from heat. Stir in ¼ cup sour cream. Cover and let stand 5 minutes.

3 Cut potatoes open. Divide beef mixture evenly among potatoes. Top with remaining ¼ cup sour cream.   *Makes 4 servings*

Ready to serve in 25 minutes.

SPICY BEEF AND ONION SANDWICHES

❖

Warm and spicy, these sandwiches are a great choice for an easy lunch. Lean beef, trimmed of excess fat, can play a part in healthful eating. It can't be beat as a source of dietary iron, which is needed to produce red blood cells.

❖

Nutrients per Serving:

Calories	347
(28% of calories from fat)	
Total Fat	11 g
Saturated Fat	3 g
Cholesterol	38 mg
Sodium	541 mg
Carbohydrate	41 g
Dietary Fiber	1 g
Protein	21 g
Calcium	104 mg
Iron	4 mg
Vitamin A	2 RE
Vitamin C	3 mg

DIETARY EXCHANGES:
2 Starch/Bread, 2 Lean
Meat, 2 Vegetable, 1 Fat

Nonstick cooking spray
6 ounces beef top sirloin steak, cut 1 inch thick
1 medium onion, thinly sliced
1 tablespoon mustard seeds
½ cup water
1 cup sliced mushrooms
1 tablespoon sugar
1 tablespoon cider vinegar
1 teaspoon olive oil
3 kaiser rolls
3 tablespoons spicy brown mustard

1 Spray large nonstick skillet with cooking spray. Heat over medium heat until hot. Add beef. Partially cover and cook 4 minutes on each side or until cooked through. Remove beef from skillet.

2 Add onion, mustard seeds and water to skillet. Cook over medium-high heat 5 minutes or until water has evaporated. Add mushrooms, sugar, vinegar and olive oil. Cook 5 minutes or until onions are browned, stirring frequently.

3 Cut rolls crosswise in half. Spread with mustard. Thinly slice meat; layer on rolls. Top with onion mixture. *Makes 3 servings*

Ready to serve in 30 minutes.

MEDITERRANEAN MEATBALLS AND COUSCOUS

❖

Couscous, a granular semolina pasta, is a staple in the cuisines of several northern African countries.

❖

Nutrients per Serving:

Calories	434
(22% of calories from fat)	
Total Fat	11 g
Saturated Fat	4 g
Cholesterol	50 mg
Sodium	180 mg
Carbohydrate	61 g
Dietary Fiber	8 g
Protein	23 g
Calcium	75 mg
Iron	3 mg
Vitamin A	15 RE
Vitamin C	6 mg

DIETARY EXCHANGES:
3 Starch/Bread, 2 Lean
Meat, 1 Fruit, 1 Fat

1 can (about 14 ounces) ⅓-less-salt chicken broth
2½ cups water
1½ cups precooked couscous*
¾ cup golden raisins
¼ cup chopped parsley
3 tablespoons fresh lemon juice, divided
3 teaspoons grated lemon peel, divided
2 teaspoons ground cinnamon, divided
1 teaspoon turmeric
½ teaspoon ground cumin
1 pound ground round beef
½ cup crushed saltine crackers
¼ cup evaporated skimmed milk
½ teaspoon dried oregano

1 Pour chicken broth and water into 2-quart saucepan. Bring to a boil over high heat. Remove from heat. Add couscous, raisins, parsley, 2 tablespoons lemon juice, 2 teaspoons lemon peel, 1½ teaspoons cinnamon, turmeric and cumin. Cover and let stand 5 minutes.

2 Combine beef, crackers, milk, remaining 1 tablespoon lemon juice, 1 teaspoon lemon peel, ½ teaspoon cinnamon and oregano in large bowl. Mix until well blended. Shape into 24 meatballs. Place in large microwavable baking dish. Cover loosely with waxed paper. Microwave at HIGH 4 minutes or until meatballs are cooked through.

3 Stir couscous mixture and spoon onto serving platter. Arrange meatballs on couscous. Garnish with lemon wedges and fresh oregano, if desired.

Makes 6 servings

Ready to serve in 25 minutes.

*Package label may not indicate couscous is precooked. Check ingredient list for "precooked semolina."

FAJITA SALAD

Nutrients per Serving:

Calories	160
(23% of calories from fat)	
Total Fat	5 g
Saturated Fat	1 g
Cholesterol	30 mg
Sodium	667 mg
Carbohydrate	20 g
Dietary Fiber	6 g
Protein	17 g
Calcium	83 mg
Iron	4 mg
Vitamin A	259 RE
Vitamin C	81 mg

DIETARY EXCHANGES:
½ Starch/Bread, 1½ Lean Meat, 2 Vegetable

6 ounces beef top sirloin steak
¼ cup fresh lime juice
2 tablespoons chopped fresh cilantro
1 clove garlic, minced
1 teaspoon chili powder
2 medium red bell peppers
1 medium onion
1 teaspoon olive oil
1 cup garbanzo beans, drained and rinsed
4 cups mixed salad greens
1 tomato, cut into wedges
1 cup salsa

1 Cut beef into strips, about 2 × 1 × ¼-inch. Place in resealable plastic food storage bag. Combine lime juice, cilantro, garlic and chili powder in small bowl. Pour over beef; seal bag. Let stand for 10 minutes, turning once.

2 Cut peppers into strips. Cut onion into slices. Heat olive oil in large nonstick skillet over medium-high heat until hot. Add peppers and onion. Cook and stir for 6 minutes or until vegetables are crisp-tender. Remove from skillet. Add beef and marinade to skillet. Cook and stir 3 minutes or until meat is cooked through. Remove from heat. Add peppers, onion and garbanzo beans to skillet; toss to coat with pan juices. Cool slightly.

3 Divide salad greens evenly among 4 serving plates. Top with beef mixture and tomato wedges. Serve with salsa. Garnish with nonfat sour cream and fresh cilantro, if desired.

Makes 4 servings

Ready to serve in 30 minutes.

PORK

POTATO AND PORK FRITTATA

Frozen hash brown potatoes are a quick and easy source of complex carbohydrates without added fat. To reduce the cholesterol in this frittata, replace the whole eggs and egg whites with 1 cup of cholesterol-free egg substitute.

12 ounces (about 3 cups) frozen shredded hash brown potatoes
1 teaspoon Cajun seasoning
4 egg whites
2 whole eggs
¼ cup 1% low fat milk
1 teaspoon dry mustard
¼ teaspoon ground black pepper
10 ounces (about 3 cups) frozen stir-fry vegetables
¾ cup chopped cooked lean pork
½ cup (2 ounces) shredded reduced fat Cheddar cheese

1 Preheat oven to 400°F. Spray baking sheet with nonstick cooking spray. Spread potatoes on baking sheet; sprinkle with Cajun seasoning. Bake 15 minutes or until potatoes are hot. Remove from oven. Reduce oven temperature to 350°F.

2 Beat egg whites, eggs, milk, mustard and pepper in small bowl. Place vegetables and ⅓ cup water in medium nonstick skillet. Cook over medium heat 5 minutes or until vegetables are crisp-tender; drain.

3 Add pork and potatoes to vegetables in skillet; stir lightly. Add egg mixture. Sprinkle with cheese. Cook over medium-low heat 5 minutes. Place skillet in 350°F oven and bake 5 minutes or until egg mixture is set and cheese is melted.

Makes 4 servings

Ready to serve in 30 minutes.

Nutrients per Serving:

Calories	251
(27% of calories from fat)	
Total Fat	7 g
Saturated Fat	3 g
Cholesterol	135 mg
Sodium	394 mg
Carbohydrate	24 g
Dietary Fiber	2 g
Protein	22 g
Calcium	155 mg
Iron	1 mg
Vitamin A	585 RE
Vitamin C	22 mg

DIETARY EXCHANGES:
1½ Starch/Bread, 2½ Lean Meat, 1 Vegetable

SPICY PORK STIR-FRY

❖

Carrots and broccoli star in this easy stir-fry. They are significant sources of beta-carotene, a vitamin A precursor. Beta-carotene has been linked to a reduced risk for heart disease, cataracts and certain cancers.

❖

Nutrients per Serving:

Calories	415
(17% of calories from fat)	
Total Fat	8 g
Saturated Fat	2 g
Cholesterol	34 mg
Sodium	266 mg
Carbohydrate	66 g
Dietary Fiber	4 g
Protein	18 g
Calcium	59 mg
Iron	4 mg
Vitamin A	1078 RE
Vitamin C	33 mg

DIETARY EXCHANGES:
4 Starch/Bread, 1½ Lean Meat, 1 Vegetable, ½ Fat

1 can (about 14 ounces) ⅓-less-salt chicken broth, divided
2 tablespoons reduced sodium soy sauce
2 tablespoons cornstarch
1 tablespoon grated orange peel
1 pork tenderloin (about 10 ounces)
2 tablespoons peanut oil, divided
1 tablespoon sesame seeds
2 cloves garlic, minced
2 cups broccoli flowerets
2 cups sliced carrots
1 teaspoon Szechuan seasoning
6 cups hot cooked rice, prepared in unsalted water

1 Combine 1½ cups chicken broth, soy sauce, cornstarch and orange peel in medium bowl until smooth. Cut pork lengthwise in half, then cut crosswise into ¼-inch slices.

2 Heat 1 tablespoon peanut oil in wok or large skillet over high heat until hot. Add pork, sesame seeds and garlic. Stir-fry 3 minutes or until pork is barely pink in center. Remove from wok.

3 Heat remaining 1 tablespoon peanut oil in wok over high heat until hot. Add broccoli, carrots, Szechuan seasoning and remaining 2 tablespoons chicken broth. Cook and stir 5 minutes or until vegetables are crisp-tender. Add pork. Stir chicken broth mixture and add to wok. Cook and stir over medium heat until sauce is thickened. Serve over rice.   *Makes 6 servings*

Ready to serve in 30 minutes.

NEW ORLEANS PORK GUMBO

❖

Gumbo, a thick, stewlike dish popular in New Orleans, includes okra, tomatoes and one or more meats or shellfish. A traditional gumbo starts with a dark roux, a mixture of flour and fat, which adds an unmistakable flavor. Reducing the amount of fat in the roux helps trim the calories and total fat in this recipe.

❖

1 pound pork loin roast
  Nonstick cooking spray
1 tablespoon margarine
2 tablespoons all-purpose flour
1 cup water
1 can (16 ounces) stewed tomatoes, undrained
1 package (10 ounces) frozen cut okra
1 package (10 ounces) frozen succotash
1 beef bouillon cube
1 teaspoon hot pepper sauce
1 teaspoon ground black pepper
1 bay leaf

1 Cut pork into ½-inch cubes. Spray large Dutch oven with cooking spray. Heat over medium heat until hot. Add pork; cook and stir 4 minutes or until pork is browned. Remove pork from Dutch oven.

2 Melt margarine in Dutch oven. Stir in flour. Cook and stir until roux is browned. Whisk in water. Add pork and remaining ingredients. Bring to a boil. Reduce heat to low and simmer 15 minutes. Remove bay leaf; discard.   *Makes 4 servings*

Ready to serve in 30 minutes.

Nutrients per Serving:

Calories	295
(30% of calories from fat)	
Total Fat	10 g
Saturated Fat	3 g
Cholesterol	45 mg
Sodium	602 mg
Carbohydrate	33 g
Dietary Fiber	7 g
Protein	21 g
Calcium	101 mg
Iron	3 mg
Vitamin A	160 RE
Vitamin C	34 mg

DIETARY EXCHANGES:
1 Starch/Bread, 2 Lean Meat, 2½ Vegetable, 1 Fat

GLAZED STUFFED PORK CHOPS

❖

This filling dish, rich in vitamin A, vitamin C, B vitamins, iron and fiber, packs an impressive nutritional punch.

❖

Nutrients per Serving:

Calories	490
(21% of calories from fat)	
Total Fat	12 g
Saturated Fat	4 g
Cholesterol	53 mg
Sodium	227 mg
Carbohydrate	73 g
Dietary Fiber	7 g
Protein	28 g
Calcium	153 mg
Iron	4 mg
Vitamin A	607 RE
Vitamin C	75 mg

DIETARY EXCHANGES:
3 Lean Meat, 4½ Fruit,
2 Vegetable

2 medium cooking apples
3 cups prepared cabbage slaw blend
¼ cup raisins
¾ cup apple cider, divided
2 tablespoons maple-flavored pancake syrup
4 teaspoons spicy brown mustard, divided
2 lean pork chops (about 6 ounces each), 1 inch thick
    Nonstick cooking spray
2 teaspoons cornstarch

1 Quarter and core apples. Chop 6 quarters; reserve remaining 2 quarters. Combine chopped apples, slaw blend, raisins, ¼ cup apple cider, syrup and 2 teaspoons mustard in large saucepan. Cover and cook over medium heat 5 minutes or until cabbage is tender.

2 Make a pocket in each pork chop by cutting horizontally through chop almost to bone. Fill each pocket with about ¼ cup cabbage-apple mixture. Keep remaining cabbage-apple mixture warm over low heat.

3 Spray medium nonstick skillet with cooking spray. Heat over medium heat until hot. Brown pork chops about 3 minutes on each side. Add ¼ cup apple cider. Reduce heat to low; cover and simmer 8 minutes or until pork is barely pink in center. Remove pork from skillet; keep warm.

4 Add liquid from remaining cabbage-apple mixture to skillet. Combine remaining ¼ cup apple cider, 2 teaspoons mustard and cornstarch in small bowl until smooth. Stir into liquid in skillet. Simmer over medium heat until thickened. Spoon glaze over chops and cabbage-apple mixture. Slice remaining 2 apple quarters; divide between servings. Garnish with fresh bay leaves, if desired.   *Makes 2 servings*

Ready to serve in 30 minutes.

CAJUN RED BEANS AND RICE

❖

This updated version of traditional Cajun red beans and rice, using reduced fat ham, has retained its spicy character. Beans, which are extremely low in fat, contain significant amounts of soluble fiber. This type of fiber may lower LDL cholesterol and blood sugar levels.

❖

1 cup converted white rice
1 can (15 ounces) red kidney beans, drained and rinsed
½ cup cubed 96% fat free ham
1½ cups water
1 can (about 14 ounces) ⅓-less-salt chicken broth
¼ cup tomato paste
1 bay leaf
1 teaspoon Cajun seasoning
⅛ teaspoon ground red pepper
½ teaspoon olive oil
1 medium green bell pepper, chopped
¾ cup chopped onion
¾ cup sliced celery
   Hot pepper sauce (optional)

1 Combine rice, beans, ham, water, chicken broth, tomato paste, bay leaf, Cajun seasoning and red pepper in large saucepan. Bring to a boil. Reduce heat to low; cover and simmer 15 minutes.

2 Meanwhile, heat olive oil in medium skillet over medium heat until hot. Add bell pepper, onion and celery. Cook and stir 5 minutes; add to rice mixture. Continue to simmer 10 minutes or until rice is tender and flavors have blended. If mixture becomes dry, add small amount of water. Remove bay leaf; discard. Serve with hot pepper sauce.   *Makes 4 servings*

Ready to serve in 30 minutes.

Nutrients per Serving:

Calories	335
(7% of calories from fat)	
Total Fat	3 g
Saturated Fat	<1 g
Cholesterol	5 mg
Sodium	611 mg
Carbohydrate	66 g
Dietary Fiber	9 g
Protein	17 g
Calcium	56 mg
Iron	3 mg
Vitamin A	58 RE
Vitamin C	32 mg

DIETARY EXCHANGES:
4 Starch/Bread, ½ Lean Meat, 1 Vegetable

HAM AND BROCCOLI CHOWDER

For a warming meal on a cold winter day, serve Ham and Broccoli Chowder with a fruit salad and hot crusty bread.

2 cups broccoli flowerets
1 cup chopped onion
2 ribs celery, sliced
¼ cup water
½ cup all-purpose flour
3 cups skim milk
1 teaspoon salt-free Italian herb blend
¼ teaspoon ground black pepper
3 ounces 97% fat free ham
½ cup (2 ounces) shredded reduced fat sharp Cheddar cheese
5 green onions, chopped

1 Combine broccoli, onion, celery and water in 2-quart microwavable container. Cover and microwave at HIGH 6 minutes, stirring halfway through cooking.

2 Whisk together flour, milk, herb blend and pepper in medium bowl. Stir into vegetables. Cover and microwave at HIGH 6 minutes or until mixture thickens and comes to a boil, stirring every 2 minutes.

3 Cut ham into ½-inch pieces. Add ham to broccoli mixture. Cover and microwave at HIGH 1 minute. Add cheese. Cover and let stand 5 minutes. Stir until cheese is melted. Serve in bowls; sprinkle with green onions.   *Makes 4 (1½-cup) servings*

Ready to serve in 30 minutes.

Nutrients per Serving:

Calories	220
(16% of calories from fat)	
Total Fat	4 g
Saturated Fat	2 g
Cholesterol	17 mg
Sodium	559 mg
Carbohydrate	29 g
Dietary Fiber	3 g
Protein	18 g
Calcium	379 mg
Iron	2 mg
Vitamin A	248 RE
Vitamin C	56 mg

DIETARY EXCHANGES:
1 Starch/Bread, 1 Lean Meat, ½ Milk,
1½ Vegetable

PORK WITH SWEET HUNGARIAN PAPRIKA

❖

Lean pork is nutrient-dense—it provides a lot of nutrients for the calories. It is an excellent source of almost all the B vitamins, which help process carbohydrates, protein and fats into energy.

❖

1 teaspoon olive oil, divided
1 onion, sliced
2 cloves garlic, minced
1 tomato, chopped
1 medium red bell pepper, chopped
1 large Anaheim or 1 medium green bell pepper, chopped
1 can (10½ ounces) ⅓-less-salt chicken broth, divided
2 tablespoons sweet Hungarian paprika
1 pork tenderloin (12 ounces)
3 tablespoons all-purpose flour
⅓ cup low fat sour cream
6 cups cooked enriched egg noodles (6 ounces uncooked)

1 Heat ½ teaspoon olive oil in medium saucepan over medium heat until hot. Add onion and garlic. Cook and stir 2 minutes. Add tomato, peppers, ½ cup chicken broth and paprika. Reduce heat to low; cover and simmer 5 minutes.

2 Cut pork crosswise into 8 slices. Pound pork between two pieces of plastic wrap to ¼-inch thickness, using flat side of meat mallet or rolling pin. Heat remaining ½ teaspoon olive oil in nonstick skillet over medium heat until hot. Cook pork 1 minute on each side or until browned. Add onion mixture. Reduce heat to low and simmer 5 minutes. Whisk together remaining chicken broth and flour in small bowl.

3 Remove pork from skillet; keep warm. Stir flour mixture into liquid in skillet. Bring liquid to a boil; remove from heat. Stir in sour cream. Serve sauce over pork and noodles. Garnish with additional sweet Hungarian paprika and parsley, if desired.

Makes 4 servings

Ready to serve in 30 minutes.

Nutrients per Serving:

Calories	380
(22% of calories from fat)	
Total Fat	9 g
Saturated Fat	2 g
Cholesterol	110 mg
Sodium	96 mg
Carbohydrate	45 g
Dietary Fiber	2 g
Protein	28 g
Calcium	99 mg
Iron	5 mg
Vitamin A	412 RE
Vitamin C	49 mg

DIETARY EXCHANGES:
2½ Starch/Bread, 3 Lean Meat, 1½ Vegetable

POULTRY

TURKEY AND BEAN TOSTADAS

6 (8-inch) flour tortillas
1 pound 93% fat free ground turkey
1 can (15 ounces) chili beans in chili sauce
½ teaspoon chili powder
3 cups shredded romaine lettuce
1 large tomato, chopped
¼ cup chopped fresh cilantro
¼ cup (1 ounce) shredded reduced fat Monterey Jack cheese
½ cup low fat sour cream (optional)

1 Preheat oven to 350°F. Place tortillas on baking sheets. Bake 7 minutes or until crisp. Place on individual plates.

2 Heat large nonstick skillet over medium-high heat until hot. Add turkey. Cook and stir until turkey is browned; drain. Add beans in sauce and chili powder. Cook 5 minutes over medium heat. Divide turkey mixture evenly among tortillas. Top with remaining ingredients. *Makes 6 servings*

Ready to serve in 20 minutes.

Replacing iceberg lettuce with romaine lettuce is a wise decision, since the darker green leaves of romaine are more nutritious.

Nutrients per Serving:

Calories 288
(30% of calories from fat)
Total Fat 10 g
Saturated Fat 2 g
Cholesterol 30 mg
Sodium 494 mg
Carbohydrate 34 g
Dietary Fiber 2 g
Protein 19 g
Calcium 151 mg
Iron 4 mg
Vitamin A 163 RE
Vitamin C 16 mg

DIETARY EXCHANGES:
1 Starch/Bread, 2 Lean Meat, 2½ Vegetable, 1 Fat

CHICKEN BREASTS WITH CRABMEAT STUFFING

❖

Whole wheat cracker crumbs provide a delicious coating for microwave-cooked chicken breasts.

❖

Nutrients per Serving:

Calories	246
(17% of calories from fat)	
Total Fat	5 g
Saturated Fat	2 g
Cholesterol	83 mg
Sodium	424 mg
Carbohydrate	21 g
Dietary Fiber	<1 g
Protein	30 g
Calcium	113 mg
Iron	2 mg
Vitamin A	67 RE
Vitamin C	6 mg

DIETARY EXCHANGES:
1½ Starch/Bread, 3 Lean Meat

4 boneless skinless chicken breast halves (about 1 pound)
¾ cup whole wheat cracker crumbs, divided
3 ounces canned crabmeat, drained and rinsed twice
¼ cup fat free mayonnaise
2 tablespoons grated Parmesan cheese
2 tablespoons finely chopped green onions
2 tablespoons fresh lemon juice
¼ teaspoon hot pepper sauce
1 tablespoon dried parsley flakes
1 teaspoon ground black pepper
1 teaspoon paprika
½ cup 1% low fat milk

1 Pound chicken breasts between two pieces of plastic wrap to ¼-inch thickness, using flat side of meat mallet or rolling pin.

2 Combine ¼ cup cracker crumbs, crabmeat, mayonnaise, cheese, onions, lemon juice and pepper sauce in medium bowl. Divide filling evenly among chicken breasts. Roll up each chicken breast from short side, tucking in ends; secure with wooden pick.

3 Combine remaining ½ cup cracker crumbs, parsley flakes, black pepper and paprika in shallow bowl. Dip chicken in milk; roll in cracker crumb mixture. Place chicken in microwavable round or square baking dish. Cover with waxed paper. Microwave at HIGH 10 minutes or until chicken is no longer pink in center. Remove chicken from dish. Remove wooden picks. Add remaining milk to pan juices; microwave at HIGH 1 minute or until sauce comes to a boil. Serve chicken with sauce.

Makes 4 servings

Ready to serve in 30 minutes.

CURRIED CHICKEN BREASTS

This showstopping curry dish is mild enough for everyone. The brown rice and fruits add flavor and fiber.

❖

1 can (10½ ounces) ⅓-less-salt chicken broth
1 tablespoon curry powder
⅓ cup all-purpose flour
½ teaspoon salt
½ teaspoon ground black pepper
4 boneless skinless chicken breast halves (about 1 pound)
2 teaspoons olive oil
1 medium onion, sliced
2 cloves garlic, minced
1 cup instant brown rice
1 cup canned pineapple chunks
1 apple, cored and sliced
¼ cup golden raisins

1 Combine chicken broth and curry powder in small bowl. Combine flour, salt and pepper in shallow bowl; coat chicken breasts lightly with flour mixture.

2 Heat olive oil in large nonstick skillet over medium heat until hot. Add chicken breasts. Cook 3 minutes on each side or until browned; remove chicken from skillet. Add chicken broth mixture, onion and garlic to skillet. Cook 5 minutes or until onion is tender, stirring occasionally. Add chicken. Reduce heat to low; cover and simmer 10 minutes or until chicken is no longer pink in center.

3 Meanwhile, cook rice according to package directions, omitting salt and butter. Spoon rice onto serving platter. Top with chicken and onion, reserving liquid in skillet. Add pineapple, apple and raisins to liquid in skillet. Cook fruits over medium heat 3 minutes or until heated through. Arrange fruits over chicken and rice.

Makes 4 servings

Ready to serve in 30 minutes.

Nutrients per Serving:

Calories	390
(14% of calories from fat)	
Total Fat	6 g
Saturated Fat	1 g
Cholesterol	46 mg
Sodium	166 mg
Carbohydrate	62 g
Dietary Fiber	3 g
Protein	23 g
Calcium	63 mg
Iron	3 mg
Vitamin A	8 RE
Vitamin C	9 mg

DIETARY EXCHANGES:
2½ Starch/Bread,
2 Lean Meat, 1½ Fruit,
½ Vegetable

SKILLET CHICKEN POT PIE

1 can (10¾ ounces) ⅓-less-salt, 99% fat free cream of chicken soup
1¼ cups skim milk, divided
1 package (10 ounces) frozen mixed vegetables
2 cups diced cooked chicken
½ teaspoon ground black pepper
1 cup buttermilk biscuit baking mix
¼ teaspoon summer savory or parsley

1 Heat soup, 1 cup milk, vegetables, chicken and pepper in medium skillet over medium heat until mixture comes to a boil.

2 Combine biscuit mix and summer savory in small bowl. Stir in 3 to 4 tablespoons milk just until soft batter is formed. Drop batter by tablespoonfuls onto chicken mixture to make 6 dumplings. Partially cover and simmer 12 minutes or until dumplings are cooked through, spooning liquid from pot pie over dumplings once or twice during cooking. Garnish with additional summer savory, if desired.

Makes 6 servings

Ready to serve in 25 minutes.

❖

Not all convenience foods are "no-no's." This recipe combines several prepared foods to give a product with "made from scratch" flavor.

❖

Nutrients per Serving:

Calories	241
(21% of calories from fat)	
Total Fat	5 g
Saturated Fat	1 g
Cholesterol	33 mg
Sodium	422 mg
Carbohydrate	25 g
Dietary Fiber	<1 g
Protein	17 g
Calcium	119 mg
Iron	2 mg
Vitamin A	248 RE
Vitamin C	8 mg

DIETARY EXCHANGES:
1 Starch/Bread, 2 Lean Meat, 1½ Vegetable

TURKEY GYROS

❖

The mild flavor of turkey blends well with a wide variety of seasonings. Here turkey tenderloin, which is quick to prepare and low in fat, replaces lamb in gyros.

❖

Nutrients per Serving:

Calories	319
(12% of calories from fat)	
Total Fat	4 g
Saturated Fat	2 g
Cholesterol	55 mg
Sodium	477 mg
Carbohydrate	42 g
Dietary Fiber	1 g
Protein	27 g
Calcium	205 mg
Iron	3 mg
Vitamin A	101 RE
Vitamin C	17 mg

DIETARY EXCHANGES:
2½ Starch/Bread, 2 Lean Meat, 1 Vegetable

1 turkey tenderloin (8 ounces)
1½ teaspoons Greek seasoning
1 cucumber
⅔ cup plain nonfat yogurt
¼ cup finely chopped onion
2 teaspoons dried dill weed
2 teaspoons fresh lemon juice
1 teaspoon olive oil
4 pita breads
1½ cups shredded romaine lettuce
1 tomato, thinly sliced
2 tablespoons crumbled feta cheese

1 Cut turkey tenderloin across the grain into ¼-inch slices. Place turkey slices on plate; lightly sprinkle both sides with Greek seasoning. Let stand 5 minutes.

2 Cut two-thirds of cucumber into thin slices. Finely chop remaining cucumber. Combine chopped cucumber, yogurt, onion, dill weed and lemon juice in small bowl.

3 Heat olive oil in large skillet over medium heat until hot. Add turkey. Cook 2 minutes on each side or until cooked through. Wrap 2 pita breads in paper towel. Microwave at HIGH 30 seconds or just until warmed. Repeat with remaining pita breads. Divide shredded lettuce, tomato, cucumber slices, turkey, feta cheese and yogurt-cucumber sauce evenly among pita breads. Fold edges over and secure with wooden picks. *Makes 4 servings*

Ready to serve in 25 minutes.

CHICKEN PASTA SALAD WITH NECTARINES AND GRAPES

❖

This appetizing salad with juicy nectarines and sweet grapes is perfect for a quick meal on a hot summer day. With 3 grams of fat per serving, there is no need to feel guilty about serving a "creamy" salad.

❖

Nutrients per Serving:

Calories	280
(8% of calories from fat)	
Total Fat	3 g
Saturated Fat	1 g
Cholesterol	35 mg
Sodium	305 mg
Carbohydrate	48 g
Dietary Fiber	2 g
Protein	19 g
Calcium	82 mg
Iron	2 mg
Vitamin A	81 RE
Vitamin C	9 mg

DIETARY EXCHANGES:
1½ Starch/Bread, 1½ Lean Meat, 1½ Fruit

Nonstick cooking spray
3 boneless skinless chicken breast halves (about 12 ounces)
1 cup uncooked pasta shells
½ cup fat free mayonnaise
½ cup plain nonfat yogurt
2 tablespoons fresh lime juice
1 tablespoon brown sugar
1 teaspoon dry mustard
1 teaspoon ground ginger
3 nectarines, coarsely chopped
1 cup green grapes

1 Spray medium nonstick skillet with cooking spray. Heat over medium heat until hot. Add chicken. Cook 3 minutes on each side or until chicken is no longer pink in center. Remove from skillet; refrigerate 10 minutes. Cut into cubes.

2 Cook pasta according to package directions, omitting salt; drain. Rinse with cold water; drain.

3 Combine mayonnaise, yogurt, lime juice, brown sugar, mustard and ginger in large bowl. Add chicken, pasta, nectarines and grapes; toss until coated with dressing. Serve on lettuce leaves, if desired. *Makes 4 servings*

Ready to serve in 25 minutes.

MANDARIN CHICKEN SALAD

❖

A refreshing salad with a light honey-soy sauce dressing. To speed preparation, buy prepared red cabbage, radishes and red onion from the salad bar.

◆

1 cup rice-flour noodles
1 can (6 ounces) mandarin orange segments, chilled
⅓ cup honey
2 tablespoons rice vinegar
2 tablespoons reduced sodium soy sauce
1 can (8 ounces) sliced water chestnuts, drained
4 cups shredded Napa cabbage
1 cup shredded red cabbage
½ cup sliced radishes
4 thin slices red onion, cut in half and separated
3 boneless skinless chicken breast halves (about 12 ounces), cooked and cut into strips

1 Place rice-flour noodles in medium bowl; cover with water. Let stand 10 minutes; drain. Drain mandarin orange segments, reserving ⅓ cup liquid. Whisk together reserved liquid, honey, vinegar and soy sauce in small bowl. Add water chestnuts.

2 Divide Napa and red cabbages, radishes and onion evenly among 4 serving plates. Top with chicken and orange segments. Remove water chestnuts from dressing and arrange on salads. Serve with rice-flour noodles; drizzle with dressing.

Makes 4 servings

Ready to serve in 20 minutes.

Nutrients per Serving:

Calories	258
(6% of calories from fat)	
Total Fat	2 g
Saturated Fat	1 g
Cholesterol	34 mg
Sodium	318 mg
Carbohydrate	46 g
Dietary Fiber	2 g
Protein	16 g
Calcium	86 mg
Iron	2 mg
Vitamin A	146 RE
Vitamin C	69 mg

DIETARY EXCHANGES:
1 Starch/Bread, 2 Lean Meat, ½ Fruit, 2 Vegetable

THAI CHICKEN PIZZA

❖

*Beta-carotene, which is
found in certain red-,
orange-, yellow- and green-
pigmented fruits and
vegetables, is converted by
the body into vitamin A.
Carrot and red pepper
combine in this recipe to
provide more than half the
Recommended Dietary
Allowance of vitamin A.*

❖

2 boneless skinless chicken breast halves (½ pound)
2 teaspoons Thai seasoning
  Nonstick cooking spray
2 tablespoons pineapple juice
1 tablespoon peanut butter
1 tablespoon oyster sauce
1 teaspoon Thai chili paste*
2 (10-inch) flour tortillas
½ cup shredded carrot
½ cup sliced green onions
½ cup red bell pepper slices
¼ cup chopped cilantro
½ cup (2 ounces) shredded part-skim mozzarella cheese

1 Preheat oven to 400°F. Cut chicken breasts crosswise into thin slices, each about 1½ × ½ inch. Sprinkle with Thai seasoning. Let stand 5 minutes. Spray large nonstick skillet with cooking spray. Heat over medium heat until hot. Add chicken. Cook and stir 3 minutes or until chicken is lightly browned and no longer pink in center.

2 Combine pineapple juice, peanut butter, oyster sauce and chili paste in small bowl until smooth. Place tortillas on baking sheets. Spread peanut butter mixture over tortillas. Divide chicken, carrot, onions, pepper and cilantro evenly between each tortilla. Sprinkle with cheese. Bake 5 minutes or until tortillas are crisp and cheese is melted. Cut into wedges. *Makes 4 servings*

Ready to serve in 25 minutes.

*Thai chili paste is available at some larger supermarkets and at Oriental markets.

Nutrients per Serving:

½ of one pizza

Calories	201
(31% of calories from fat)	
Total Fat	7 g
Saturated Fat	2 g
Cholesterol	38 mg
Sodium	556 mg
Carbohydrate	17 g
Dietary Fiber	1 g
Protein	18 g
Calcium	140 mg
Iron	2 mg
Vitamin A	655 RE
Vitamin C	71 mg

DIETARY EXCHANGES:
1 Starch/Bread, 2 Lean
Meat, ½ Vegetable

CONFETTI CHICKEN CHILI

Chili made with chicken and white beans may be lighter in color, but it's rich with protein and flavor. Colorful, confettilike vegetables supply eye appeal and their share of nutrients, too.

1 pound 90% fat free ground chicken or 93% fat free ground turkey
1 large onion, chopped
2 carrots, chopped
2 plum tomatoes, chopped
1 large Anaheim or 1 medium green bell pepper, chopped
1 jalapeño pepper, finely chopped*
1 can (15 ounces) Great Northern beans, drained and rinsed
2 cans (about 14 ounces each) ⅓-less-salt chicken broth
2 teaspoons chili powder
½ teaspoon ground red pepper

1 Heat large nonstick saucepan over medium heat until hot. Add chicken and onion; cook and stir 5 minutes or until chicken is browned. Drain fat from saucepan.

2 Add remaining ingredients to saucepan. Bring to a boil. Reduce heat to low and simmer 15 minutes.   *Makes 5 servings*

Ready to serve in 30 minutes.

*Jalapeño peppers can sting and irritate the skin; wear rubber gloves when handling peppers and do not touch your eyes. Wash your hands after handling jalapeño peppers.

Nutrients per Serving:

Calories	282
(28% of calories from fat)	
Total Fat	9 g
Saturated Fat	3 g
Cholesterol	67 mg
Sodium	136 mg
Carbohydrate	28 g
Dietary Fiber	3 g
Protein	25 g
Calcium	95 mg
Iron	4 mg
Vitamin A	887 RE
Vitamin C	31 mg

DIETARY EXCHANGES:
1 Starch/Bread, 2½ Lean Meat, 2 Vegetable, ½ Fat

SEAFOOD

BROILED TUNA AND RASPBERRY SALAD

Raspberry vinegar and fresh raspberries add vibrant flavor and color to this refreshing salad.

½ cup commercial fat free ranch salad dressing
¼ cup raspberry vinegar
1½ teaspoons Cajun seasoning
1 thick-sliced tuna steak (about 6 to 8 ounces)
2 cups washed and torn romaine lettuce leaves
1 cup washed and torn mixed baby lettuce leaves
½ cup fresh raspberries

1 Combine salad dressing, vinegar and Cajun seasoning in small bowl. Pour ¼ cup salad dressing mixture into resealable plastic food storage bag to use as marinade, reserving remaining mixture. Add tuna to marinade. Seal bag; turn to coat tuna. Marinate in refrigerator 10 minutes, turning once.

2 Preheat broiler. Spray rack of broiler pan with nonstick cooking spray. Place tuna on rack. Broil, 4 inches from heat, 5 minutes. Turn and brush with marinade; discard remaining marinade. Broil 5 minutes more or until tuna flakes in center. Cool 5 minutes. Cut into ¼-inch slices.

3 Toss together lettuces in large bowl; divide evenly between 2 serving plates. Top with tuna and raspberries; drizzle with reserved salad dressing mixture.

Makes 2 servings

Ready to serve in 30 minutes.

Nutrients per Serving:

Calories	215
(22% of calories from fat)	
Total Fat	5 g
Saturated Fat	1 g
Cholesterol	35 mg
Sodium	427 mg
Carbohydrate	18 g
Dietary Fiber	5 g
Protein	24 g
Calcium	42 mg
Iron	3 mg
Vitamin A	982 RE
Vitamin C	71 mg

DIETARY EXCHANGES:
3 Lean Meat, ½ Fruit,
1 Vegetable

RED SNAPPER VERA CRUZ

Bursting with flavor but low in total fat, saturated fat and sodium, this south-of-the-border dish is a breeze to make.

Nutrients per Serving:

Calories	144
(12% of calories from fat)	
Total Fat	2 g
Saturated Fat	<1 g
Cholesterol	42 mg
Sodium	61 mg
Carbohydrate	7 g
Dietary Fiber	2 g
Protein	24 g
Calcium	48 mg
Iron	1 mg
Vitamin A	103 RE
Vitamin C	65 mg

DIETARY EXCHANGES:
2½ Lean Meat, 1 Vegetable

4 red snapper fillets (4 ounces each)
¼ cup fresh lime juice
1 tablespoon fresh lemon juice
1 teaspoon chili powder
4 green onions with 4 inches of tops, sliced in ½-inch lengths
1 tomato, coarsely chopped
½ cup chopped Anaheim or green bell pepper
½ cup chopped red bell pepper

1 Place red snapper in shallow microwavable baking dish. Combine lime juice, lemon juice and chili powder in measuring cup. Pour over snapper. Marinate 10 minutes, turning once or twice.

2 Sprinkle onions, tomato and peppers over snapper. Cover dish loosely with plastic wrap. Microwave at HIGH 6 minutes or just until snapper flakes in center, rotating dish every 2 minutes. Let stand, covered, 4 minutes before serving. Garnish with fresh cilantro.

Makes 4 servings

Ready to serve in 25 minutes.

❖

Cook's Tip

To preserve moistness in lean fish such as cod, haddock, red snapper and sole, cook only until the thickest part turns opaque and flakes when touched with a fork.

❖

STIR-FRY SHRIMP AND SNOW PEAS

❖

Rice is a good source of complex carbohydrates and contains virtually no fat.

❖

¾ cup ⅓-less-salt chicken broth
1 tablespoon oyster sauce
1 teaspoon rice vinegar
1 tablespoon cornstarch
½ teaspoon sugar
2 teaspoons peanut oil
1 small red onion, cut into thin wedges
1 teaspoon minced fresh ginger
1 clove garlic, minced
½ pound medium shrimp, peeled and deveined
2 cups snow peas, cut diagonally into 1-inch lengths
3 cups hot cooked rice, prepared in unsalted water

1 Blend chicken broth, oyster sauce and rice vinegar into cornstarch and sugar in small bowl until smooth.

2 Heat peanut oil in wok or large nonstick skillet over medium heat until hot. Add onion, ginger and garlic; stir-fry 2 minutes. Add shrimp and snow peas. Stir-fry 3 minutes or until shrimp are opaque.

3 Stir chicken broth mixture and add to wok. Cook 1 minute or until sauce comes to a boil and thickens. Serve over rice. *Makes 4 servings*

Ready to serve in 25 minutes.

MAHI-MAHI WITH FRESH PINEAPPLE SALSA

❖

The pineapple salsa, which is rich in vitamin C, may be prepared 1 to 2 days ahead and refrigerated in an airtight container.

❖

Nutrients per Serving:

Calories	168
(24% of calories from fat)	
Total Fat	5 g
Saturated Fat	1 g
Cholesterol	83 mg
Sodium	102 mg
Carbohydrate	10 g
Dietary Fiber	1 g
Protein	22 g
Calcium	12 mg
Iron	2 mg
Vitamin A	118 RE
Vitamin C	58 mg

DIETARY EXCHANGES:
2½ Lean Meat, ½ Fruit

1½ cups diced fresh pineapple
¼ cup finely chopped red bell pepper
¼ cup finely chopped green bell pepper
2 tablespoons chopped fresh cilantro
2 tablespoons fresh lime juice, divided
½ teaspoon crushed red pepper flakes
½ teaspoon grated lime peel
4 mahi-mahi fillets (4 ounces each)
1 tablespoon olive oil
½ teaspoon ground white pepper

1 To prepare Pineapple Salsa, combine pineapple, bell peppers, cilantro, 1 tablespoon lime juice, red pepper flakes and lime peel in medium bowl.

2 Preheat broiler. Spray rack of broiler pan with nonstick cooking spray. Rinse mahi-mahi; pat dry. Place mahi-mahi on rack. Combine remaining 1 tablespoon lime juice and olive oil; brush on mahi-mahi.

3 Broil, 4 inches from heat, 3 to 4 minutes. Turn and brush with olive oil mixture; sprinkle with white pepper. Continue to broil 3 to 4 minutes or until mahi-mahi flakes in center. Serve with Pineapple Salsa. *Makes 4 servings*

Ready to serve in 30 minutes.

CIOPPINO

Nutrients per Serving:

Calories	122
(18% of calories from fat)	
Total Fat	2 g
Saturated Fat	<1 g
Cholesterol	75 mg
Sodium	412 mg
Carbohydrate	8 g
Dietary Fiber	2 g
Protein	18 g
Calcium	90 mg
Iron	2 mg
Vitamin A	53 RE
Vitamin C	16 mg

DIETARY EXCHANGES:
2 Lean Meat, 1 Vegetable

1 teaspoon olive oil
1 large onion, chopped
1 cup sliced celery, with celery tops
1 clove garlic, minced
4 cups water
1 fish flavor bouillon cube
1 tablespoon salt free Italian herb seasoning
¼ pound cod or other boneless mild-flavored fish fillets
¼ pound small shrimp, peeled and deveined
¼ pound bay scallops
1 large tomato, chopped
¼ cup flaked crabmeat or crabmeat blend
1 can (10 ounces) baby clams, drained and rinsed (optional)
2 tablespoons fresh lemon juice

1 Heat olive oil in large saucepan over medium heat until hot. Add onion, celery and garlic. Cook and stir 5 minutes or until onion is tender. Add water, bouillon cube and Italian seasoning. Cover and bring to a boil over high heat.

2 Cut cod fillets into ½-inch pieces. Add cod, shrimp, scallops and tomato to saucepan. Reduce heat to medium-low; simmer 10 to 15 minutes or until seafood is opaque. Add crabmeat, clams and lemon juice. Heat through.   *Makes 4 servings*

Ready to serve in 30 minutes.

TUNA CURRY PASTA SALAD

❖

This salad with its mild curry flavor is a quick meal to fix for spur-of-the-moment entertaining. The nutritional profile is excellent, providing a substantial amount of vitamin A, B vitamins and iron.

❖

2 cups uncooked rotini pasta
½ cup plain nonfat yogurt
½ cup reduced fat mayonnaise
2 tablespoons commercial reduced calorie Italian salad dressing
1 tablespoon mild curry powder
2 teaspoons fresh lemon juice
1 can (8 ounces) sliced water chestnuts, drained
1 small carrot, shredded
⅓ cup raisins
1 can (6 ounces) water-packed white tuna, drained and flaked
4 cups mixed salad greens
1 medium tomato, cut in wedges
1 small cucumber, sliced

1 Cook rotini according to package directions, omitting salt; drain. Rinse with cold water; drain.

2 Combine yogurt, mayonnaise, salad dressing, curry powder and lemon juice in large bowl. Add rotini, water chestnuts, carrot, raisins and tuna; toss to coat evenly.

3 Divide salad greens evenly among 4 serving plates. Top with tuna mixture, tomato and cucumber.   *Makes 4 servings*

Ready to serve in 15 minutes.

Nutrients per Serving:

Calories	454
(21% of calories from fat)	
Total Fat	11 g
Saturated Fat	3 g
Cholesterol	19 mg
Sodium	550 mg
Carbohydrate	68 g
Dietary Fiber	3 g
Protein	23 g
Calcium	125 mg
Iron	5 mg
Vitamin A	694 RE
Vitamin C	23 mg

DIETARY EXCHANGES:
3 Starch/Bread, 1 Lean Meat, ½ Fruit, 3 Vegetable, 2 Fat

HAWAIIAN SHRIMP KABOBS

❖

These colorful, low-in-fat kabobs are the perfect choice for easy summer entertaining.

❖

Nutrients per Serving:

2 kabobs

Calories	213
(5% of calories from fat)	
Total Fat	1 g
Saturated Fat	<1 g
Cholesterol	139 mg
Sodium	273 mg
Carbohydrate	35 g
Dietary Fiber	2 g
Protein	17 g
Calcium	64 mg
Iron	3 mg
Vitamin A	293 RE
Vitamin C	72 mg

DIETARY EXCHANGES:
2 Lean Meat, 1½ Fruit,
1 Vegetable

1 can (6 ounces) pineapple juice
⅓ cup brown sugar
4 teaspoons cornstarch
1 tablespoon rice vinegar
1 tablespoon reduced sodium soy sauce
1 clove garlic, minced
¼ teaspoon ground ginger
1 medium green bell pepper
1 medium red bell pepper
1 medium onion
1 cup fresh pineapple chunks
1 cup fresh mango or papaya, peeled and cut into chunks
1 pound large shrimp, peeled and deveined
2½ cups hot cooked rice, prepared in unsalted water

1 Combine pineapple juice, brown sugar, cornstarch, vinegar, soy sauce, garlic and ginger in saucepan. Cook over medium-high heat until mixture comes to a boil and thickens, stirring frequently.

2 Preheat broiler. Cut peppers and onion into 1-inch squares. Alternately thread vegetables, fruits and shrimp onto 10 metal skewers. Place kabobs in large glass baking dish. Brush sauce over kabobs.

3 Spray rack of broiler pan with nonstick cooking spray. Place kabobs on rack. Broil, 3 to 4 inches from heat, 3 minutes. Turn and brush with sauce; continue to broil 3 minutes or until shrimp are opaque. Serve with rice. Garnish with red onion rings and fresh herbs, if desired.

Makes 5 servings

Ready to serve in 30 minutes.

HERBED HADDOCK FILLETS

Any firm, white, lean fish, such as sea bass or halibut, may be used in place of haddock.

Nutrients per Serving:

Calories	221
(23% of calories from fat)	
Total Fat	6 g
Saturated Fat	1 g
Cholesterol	84 mg
Sodium	247 mg
Carbohydrate	12 g
Dietary Fiber	3 g
Protein	31 g
Calcium	139 mg
Iron	4 mg
Vitamin A	96 RE
Vitamin C	10 mg

DIETARY EXCHANGES:
½ Starch/Bread, 3½ Lean Meat

3 slices whole wheat bread
1 clove garlic
6 chive stems
½ cup loosely packed fresh parsley
¼ cup loosely packed fresh basil
2 tablespoons fresh oregano
3 to 4 tablespoons plain nonfat yogurt
1 tablespoon olive oil
1 teaspoon Dijon mustard
4 haddock fillets (5 to 6 ounces each)

1 Preheat oven to 400°F. Tear bread into pieces. Place in food processor or blender. Process until fine crumbs are formed. Measure 1 cup crumbs and place in medium bowl.

2 Place garlic in food processor or blender. Process until minced. Add chives, parsley, basil and oregano. Process until chopped, scraping sides of bowl if necessary. Add herbs to bread crumbs.

3 Combine 3 tablespoons yogurt, olive oil and mustard in small bowl. Stir into bread crumb mixture. Stir until blended and soft ball is formed. If mixture is dry, add additional 1 tablespoon yogurt.

4 Line baking sheet with foil. Place haddock on foil. Spread herb mixture over fillets. Bake 15 minutes or until fish flakes in center.   *Makes 4 servings*

Ready to serve in 30 minutes.

SCALLOPS AND MARINARA SAUCE ON SPINACH FETTUCCINE

❖

Quick-cooking scallops require no preparation. They are high in protein and low in fat—a perfect combination.

❖

Nutrients per Serving:

Calories	350
(19% of calories from fat)	
Total Fat	8 g
Saturated Fat	1 g
Cholesterol	42 mg
Sodium	470 mg
Carbohydrate	48 g
Dietary Fiber	2 g
Protein	24 g
Calcium	108 mg
Iron	2 mg
Vitamin A	91 RE
Vitamin C	36 mg

DIETARY EXCHANGES:
2 Starch/Bread, 3 Lean
Meat, 1½ Vegetable

3 teaspoons olive oil, divided
1 cup chopped onion
1 cup sliced mushrooms
1 medium red bell pepper, chopped
1 can (14½ ounces) Italian-style stewed tomatoes, undrained
½ teaspoon Thai chili paste* (optional)
9 ounces fresh uncooked spinach fettuccine
12 ounces scallops, rinsed and drained
2 tablespoons freshly grated Parmesan cheese
2 teaspoons chopped chives

1 For Marinara Sauce, heat 1 teaspoon olive oil in medium saucepan over medium heat until hot. Add onion. Cook and stir 3 minutes or until onion is tender. Add mushrooms, pepper, tomatoes and chili paste. Bring to a boil over high heat. Reduce heat to low. Cover and simmer 15 minutes, stirring occasionally.

2 Cook fettuccine according to package directions, omitting salt. Drain; keep warm. Meanwhile, heat remaining 2 teaspoons olive oil in large nonstick skillet over medium heat until hot. Add scallops. Cook and stir 4 minutes or until scallops are opaque.

3 Divide fettuccine evenly among 4 serving plates. Top with marinara sauce and scallops. Sprinkle with cheese and chives.   *Makes 4 servings*

Ready to serve in 30 minutes.

*Thai chili paste is available at some larger supermarkets and at Oriental markets.

SALMON WITH DILL-MUSTARD SAUCE

❖

Although salmon is a moderately oily fish, it is prepared here with no added fat. Therefore, the percentage of calories from fat is under 30%.

❖

Nutrients per Serving:

Calories	146
(26% of calories from fat)	
Total Fat	4 g
Saturated Fat	1 g
Cholesterol	59 mg
Sodium	253 mg
Carbohydrate	4 g
Dietary Fiber	<1 g
Protein	23 g
Calcium	17 mg
Iron	1 mg
Vitamin A	40 RE
Vitamin C	2 mg

DIETARY EXCHANGES:
3 Lean Meat

2 tablespoons fresh lemon juice
2 tablespoons fresh lime juice
4 salmon fillets (8 ounces each)
¼ cup fat free mayonnaise
1 tablespoon Dijon mustard
1 tablespoon chopped fresh dill

1 Combine lemon juice and lime juice in glass baking dish. Rinse salmon; pat dry. Place salmon in juices; marinate 10 minutes, turning once.

2 Combine mayonnaise, mustard and 1 tablespoon dill in small bowl.

3 Preheat broiler. Spray rack of broiler pan with nonstick cooking spray. Remove salmon from juices; discard juices. Pat dry. Place salmon on rack. Broil, 4 inches from heat, 3 to 4 minutes on each side or until salmon flakes in center. Serve salmon with sauce. Garnish with fresh dill, if desired. *Makes 4 servings*

Ready to serve in 20 minutes.

❖
Health Note
Omega-3 fatty acids, which are found in fish and shellfish, may reduce the risk of heart disease by lowering total blood cholesterol.
❖

CRAB AND PASTA SALAD IN CANTALOUPE

❖

The fruits in this salad provide plenty of vitamin C—almost half of the Recommended Dietary Allowance. Vitamin C has antioxidant properties that may reduce the risk of heart disease and cancer. Antioxidants also protect cells from damage from free radicals.

❖

1½ cups uncooked rotini pasta
1 cup seedless green grapes
½ cup chopped celery
½ cup fresh pineapple chunks
1 small red onion, coarsely chopped
6 ounces canned, fresh or frozen crabmeat, drained and rinsed
½ cup plain nonfat yogurt
¼ cup whipped salad dressing
2 tablespoons fresh lemon juice
2 tablespoons honey
2 teaspoons grated lemon peel
1 teaspoon Dijon mustard
2 small cantaloupes

1 Cook rotini according to package directions, omitting salt; drain. Rinse with cold water; drain.

2 Combine grapes, celery, pineapple, onion and crabmeat in large bowl. Combine yogurt, salad dressing, lemon juice, honey, lemon peel and mustard in small bowl. Add yogurt mixture and pasta to crabmeat mixture. Toss to coat evenly. Cover and refrigerate.

3 Cut cantaloupes in half. Remove and discard seeds. Remove some of cantaloupe with spoon, leaving a shell about ¾ inch thick. Fill cantaloupe halves with salad.

Makes 4 servings

Ready to serve in 20 minutes.

Nutrients per Serving:

Calories	331
(17% of calories from fat)	
Total Fat	6 g
Saturated Fat	1 g
Cholesterol	42 mg
Sodium	463 mg
Carbohydrate	56 g
Dietary Fiber	1 g
Protein	14 g
Calcium	105 mg
Iron	2 mg
Vitamin A	119 RE
Vitamin C	26 mg

DIETARY EXCHANGES:
1½ Starch/Bread, 1½ Lean Meat, 1½ Fruit,
½ Vegetable, 1 Fat

MEATLESS

PASTA PRIMAVERA WITH RICOTTA AND HERBS

❖

High in complex carbohydrates and low in fat, pasta can be an important part of a healthful diet if it is not combined with high-fat sauces. Here it is teamed with lots of vegetables and reduced fat ricotta cheese.

❖

Nutrients per Serving:

Calories	372
(28% of calories from fat)	
Total Fat	12 g
Saturated Fat	4 g
Cholesterol	20 mg
Sodium	301 mg
Carbohydrate	47 g
Dietary Fiber	7 g
Protein	21 g
Calcium	333 mg
Iron	3 mg
Vitamin A	196 RE
Vitamin C	64 mg

DIETARY EXCHANGES:
2½ Starch/Bread, 1 Lean
Meat, 2 Vegetable, 2 Fat

6 ounces uncooked fettuccine
1 cup reduced fat ricotta cheese
½ cup 1% low fat milk
4 teaspoons olive oil
1 clove garlic, minced
½ teaspoon crushed red pepper flakes
1½ cups sliced yellow squash
1½ cups sliced zucchini
1 cup red bell pepper strips
1 cup fresh or frozen peas
1 teaspoon salt free Italian herb blend
½ cup freshly grated Parmesan cheese

1 Cook fettuccine according to package directions, omitting salt. Drain; keep warm. Whisk together ricotta and milk in small bowl.

2 Heat olive oil in large nonstick skillet over medium heat until hot. Add garlic and red pepper flakes. Cook and stir 1 minute. Add yellow squash, zucchini, bell pepper, peas and herb blend. Cook and stir 5 minutes or until vegetables are crisp-tender.

3 Combine fettuccine, vegetables and ricotta cheese mixture in large bowl. Toss to coat evenly. Sprinkle with Parmesan cheese. *Makes 4 servings*

Ready to serve in 25 minutes.

HOT GAZPACHO BEAN SOUP

❖

This unique, hot version of gazpacho features two kinds of beans, which together provide a whopping 11 grams of fiber! In addition, the vegetables contribute more than a full day's supply of vitamin C.

❖

Nutrients per Serving:

Calories	239
(13% of calories from fat)	
Total Fat	4 g
Saturated Fat	<1 g
Cholesterol	<1 mg
Sodium	624 mg
Carbohydrate	46 g
Dietary Fiber	11 g
Protein	14 g
Calcium	38 mg
Iron	1 mg
Vitamin A	269 RE
Vitamin C	80 mg

DIETARY EXCHANGES:
1½ Starch/Bread, 1 Lean Meat, 2½ Vegetable, ½ Fat

1 tablespoon olive oil
1 cup chopped onion
1 cup chopped green bell pepper
1 clove garlic, minced
2 cans (11½ ounces each) no-salt-added vegetable juice
1 can (15 ounces) red kidney beans, drained and rinsed
1 can (15 ounces) garbanzo beans, drained and rinsed
2 beef bouillon cubes
2 tablespoons fresh lemon juice
¼ teaspoon crushed red pepper flakes
3 cups chopped tomatoes, divided
1 cup chopped cucumber
½ cup chopped green onions
½ cup plain salad croutons

1 Heat olive oil in large saucepan over medium-high heat until hot. Add onion, bell pepper and garlic. Cook 3 minutes or until vegetables are crisp-tender.

2 Add vegetable juice, beans, bouillon cubes, lemon juice, red pepper flakes and 1½ cups tomatoes. Bring to a boil. Reduce heat to low. Cover and simmer 5 minutes.

3 Divide bean mixture evenly among 6 serving bowls. Top with remaining tomatoes, cucumber, green onions and croutons.   *Makes 6 servings*

Ready to serve in 30 minutes.

BROCCOLI AND CHEESE TOPPED POTATOES

❖

Milk and three kinds of cheese make this meatless recipe rich in calcium. Calcium is necessary for building bone mass in children and young adults and is essential for preventing bone thinning in older adults. By using reduced fat and nonfat dairy products, the percentage of calories from fat is a modest 22%.

❖

4 large baking potatoes (6 to 8 ounces each)
2 cups broccoli flowerets
1 cup skim milk
½ cup nonfat cottage cheese
1 teaspoon dry mustard
½ teaspoon crushed red pepper flakes
1 cup (4 ounces) shredded reduced fat sharp Cheddar cheese, divided
1 cup (4 ounces) shredded part-skim mozzarella cheese
2 tablespoons all-purpose flour

1 Pierce potatoes in several places with fork. Place in microwave oven on paper towel. Microwave potatoes at HIGH 15 minutes or until softened. Wrap in paper towels; let stand 5 minutes.

2 Bring 1 cup water to a boil in medium saucepan over medium heat. Add broccoli. Cook 5 minutes or until broccoli is crisp-tender. Drain and discard water. Add milk, cottage cheese, mustard and red pepper flakes to broccoli in saucepan. Bring to a boil. Remove from heat; reduce heat to medium-low.

3 Combine ¾ cup Cheddar, mozzarella and flour in medium bowl. Toss to coat cheeses with flour; add to broccoli mixture. Cook and stir over medium-low heat until cheeses are melted and mixture is thickened.

4 Cut potatoes open. Divide broccoli mixture evenly among potatoes. Sprinkle with remaining ¼ cup Cheddar cheese. *Makes 4 servings*

Ready to serve in 25 minutes.

Nutrients per Serving:

Calories	381
(22% of calories from fat)	
Total Fat	9 g
Saturated Fat	5 g
Cholesterol	33 mg
Sodium	647 mg
Carbohydrate	51 g
Dietary Fiber	2 g
Protein	24 g
Calcium	509 mg
Iron	1 mg
Vitamin A	226 RE
Vitamin C	67 mg

DIETARY EXCHANGES:
3 Starch/Bread, 2 Lean Meat, 1 Vegetable, ½ Fat

PEPPER PITA PIZZAS

❖

This meatless pizza features a crust of pita bread, a Middle Eastern flat bread. Choose whole wheat pita bread for more fiber and B vitamins.

❖

1 teaspoon olive oil
1 medium onion, thinly sliced
1 medium red bell pepper, cut in thin strips
1 medium green bell pepper, cut in thin strips
4 cloves garlic, minced
2 tablespoons minced fresh basil *or* 2 teaspoons dried basil
1 tablespoon minced fresh oregano *or* 1 teaspoon dried oregano
2 plum tomatoes, coarsely chopped
4 pita breads
1 cup (4 ounces) shredded reduced fat Monterey Jack cheese

1 Preheat oven to 425°F. Heat olive oil in medium nonstick skillet over medium heat until hot. Add onion, peppers, garlic, basil and oregano. Partially cover and cook 5 minutes or until vegetables are tender, stirring occasionally. Add tomatoes. Partially cover and cook 3 minutes.

2 Place pita breads on baking sheet. Divide tomato mixture evenly among pita breads. Top each pita bread with ¼ cup cheese. Bake 5 minutes or until cheese is melted.

Makes 4 servings

Ready to serve in 30 minutes.

Nutrients per Serving:

Calories	302
(22% of calories from fat)	
Total Fat	7 g
Saturated Fat	3 g
Cholesterol	20 mg
Sodium	552 mg
Carbohydrate	44 g
Dietary Fiber	2 g
Protein	16 g
Calcium	334 mg
Iron	2 mg
Vitamin A	248 RE
Vitamin C	79 mg

DIETARY EXCHANGES:
2 Starch/Bread, 1½ Lean Meat, 2 Vegetable, ½ Fat

SPICY ORZO AND BLACK BEAN SALAD

❖

This meatless entrée salad is packed with fiber and lots of nutrients, including iron and vitamin C. Iron, which is needed to produce red blood cells, is more easily absorbed when consumed with vitamin C.

❖

Nutrients per Serving:

Calories	356
(20% of calories from fat)	
Total Fat	9 g
Saturated Fat	1 g
Cholesterol	0 mg
Sodium	467 mg
Carbohydrate	61 g
Dietary Fiber	10 g
Protein	17 g
Calcium	86 mg
Iron	4 mg
Vitamin A	20 RE
Vitamin C	35 mg

DIETARY EXCHANGES:
3½ Starch/Bread,
2 Vegetable, 1½ Fat

2 tablespoons olive oil
2 tablespoons minced jalapeño pepper,* divided
1 teaspoon chili powder
¾ cup uncooked orzo pasta
1 cup frozen mixed vegetables
1 can (16 ounces) black beans, drained and rinsed
2 thin slices red onion
¼ cup chopped cilantro
¼ cup fresh lime juice
¼ cup fresh lemon juice
4 cups washed and torn spinach leaves
2 tablespoons crumbled blue cheese (optional)

1 Combine olive oil, 1 tablespoon jalapeño and chili powder in large bowl.

2 Bring 6 cups water and remaining 1 tablespoon jalapeño to a boil in large saucepan. Add orzo. Cook 10 to 12 minutes or until tender; drain. Rinse with cold water; drain.

3 Place frozen vegetables in small microwavable container. Cover and microwave at HIGH 3 minutes or until hot; let stand 5 minutes.

4 Add orzo, vegetables, black beans, onion, cilantro, lime juice and lemon juice to olive oil mixture in bowl; stir to blend. Divide spinach evenly among 4 serving plates. Top with orzo and bean mixture. Sprinkle with blue cheese. Garnish with fresh cilantro, if desired.   *Makes 4 servings*

Ready to serve in 25 minutes.

*Jalapeño peppers can sting and irritate the skin; wear rubber gloves when handling peppers and do not touch your eyes. Wash your hands after handling jalapeño peppers.

HUMMUS PITA SANDWICHES

❖

Hummus, made of mashed, cooked garbanzo beans, has Mediterranean origins. Although hummus is used as a protein-packed sandwich spread in this recipe, it is also a healthful dip for crudites or wedges of toasted pita bread.

❖

Nutrients per Serving:

2 pita bread halves

Calories	364
(21% of calories from fat)	
Total Fat	9 g
Saturated Fat	2 g
Cholesterol	7 mg
Sodium	483 mg
Carbohydrate	59 g
Dietary Fiber	8 g
Protein	18 g
Calcium	115 mg
Iron	3 mg
Vitamin A	75 RE
Vitamin C	25 mg

DIETARY EXCHANGES:
3½ Starch/Bread,
1 Vegetable, 2 Fat

2 tablespoons sesame seeds
1 can (15 ounces) garbanzo beans
1 to 2 cloves garlic, peeled
¼ cup loosely packed parsley
3 tablespoons fresh lemon juice
1 tablespoon olive oil
¼ teaspoon ground black pepper
4 pita breads
2 tomatoes, thinly sliced
1 cucumber, sliced
1 cup alfalfa sprouts, drained and rinsed
2 tablespoons crumbled feta cheese

1 Toast sesame seeds in small nonstick skillet over medium heat 2 to 3 minutes or until lightly browned, stirring frequently. Remove from skillet and cool. Drain garbanzo beans; reserve liquid.

2 For Hummus, place garlic in food processor. Process until minced. Add garbanzo beans, parsley, lemon juice, olive oil and pepper. Process until almost smooth, scraping side of bowl once. If mixture is very thick, add 1 to 2 tablespoons reserved garbanzo bean liquid. Pour hummus into medium bowl. Stir in sesame seeds.

3 Cut pita breads in half. Spread about 3 tablespoons hummus in each pita bread half. Divide tomatoes, cucumber and alfalfa sprouts evenly among pita bread halves. Sprinkle with feta cheese.

Makes 4 servings

Ready to serve in 20 minutes.

CHEESE AND BEAN QUESADILLAS

❖

Beans are an excellent source of fiber and are high in carbohydrates. The refried beans in this recipe, made from canned pinto beans, are prepared without the traditional fat.

❖

1 can (15 ounces) pinto beans, drained and rinsed
½ cup salsa
1 teaspoon chili powder
4 (10-inch) flour tortillas
1 cup (4 ounces) shredded low sodium, reduced fat Monterey Jack cheese
¼ cup chopped fresh cilantro
¼ cup low fat sour cream

1 Place beans in medium saucepan. Mash beans with potato masher or fork. Stir in salsa and chili powder. Cook and stir over medium heat until bubbly. Reduce heat to low. Simmer 5 minutes, adding more salsa if mixture becomes dry.

2 Spray griddle with nonstick cooking spray. Heat over medium heat until hot. Brush 1 tortilla lightly on both sides with water. Heat on griddle until lightly browned. Turn tortilla. Spread with half the bean mixture; sprinkle with ½ cup cheese and 2 tablespoons cilantro. Top with a second tortilla and press lightly. Brush top of tortilla with water. Carefully turn quesadilla to brown and crisp second side. Remove from heat; repeat with remaining tortillas. Cut each quesadilla into 6 wedges. Serve with sour cream. Garnish with fresh cilantro, if desired. *Makes 6 servings*

Ready to serve in 20 minutes.

Nutrients per Serving:

2 wedges

Calories	187
(21% of calories from fat)	
Total Fat	4 g
Saturated Fat	2 g
Cholesterol	11 mg
Sodium	570 mg
Carbohydrate	25 g
Dietary Fiber	1 g
Protein	12 g
Calcium	264 mg
Iron	2 mg
Vitamin A	95 RE
Vitamin C	10 mg

DIETARY EXCHANGES:
1½ Starch/Bread, 1½ Lean Meat

Personalized Nutrition Reference for Different Calorie Levels*

Daily Calorie Level	1,600	2,000	2,200	2,800
Total Fat	53 g	65 g	73 g	93 g
% of Calories from Fat	30%	30%	30%	30%
Saturated Fat	18 g	20 g	24 g	31 g
Carbohydrate	240 g	300 g	330 g	420 g
Protein	46 g**	50 g	55 g	70 g
Dietary Fiber	20 g***	25 g	25 g	32 g
Cholesterol	300 mg	300 mg	300 mg	300 mg
Sodium	2,400 mg	2,400 mg	2,400 mg	2,400 mg
Calcium	1,000 mg	1,000 mg	1,000 mg	1,000 mg
Iron	18 mg	18 mg	18 mg	18 mg
Vitamin A	1,000 RE	1,000 RE	1,000 RE	1,000 RE
Vitamin C	60 mg	60 mg	60 mg	60 mg

* Numbers may be rounded.
** 46 g is the minimum amount of protein recommended for all calorie levels below 1,800.
*** 20 g is the minimum amount of fiber recommended for all calorie levels below 2,000.

Note: These calorie levels may not apply to children or adolescents, who have varying calorie requirements. For specific advice concerning calorie levels, please consult a registered dietitian, qualified health professional or pediatrician.

VOLUME MEASUREMENTS (dry)

⅛ teaspoon = 0.5 mL
¼ teaspoon = 1 mL
½ teaspoon = 2 mL
¾ teaspoon = 4 mL
1 teaspoon = 5 mL
1 tablespoon = 15 mL
2 tablespoons = 30 mL
¼ cup = 60 mL
⅓ cup = 75 mL
½ cup = 125 mL
⅔ cup = 150 mL
¾ cup = 175 mL
1 cup = 250 mL
2 cups = 1 pint = 500 mL
3 cups = 750 mL
4 cups = 1 quart = 1 L

VOLUME MEASUREMENTS (fluid)

1 fluid ounce (2 tablespoons) = 30 mL
4 fluid ounces (½ cup) = 125 mL
8 fluid ounces (1 cup) = 250 mL
12 fluid ounces (1½ cups) = 375 mL
16 fluid ounces (2 cups) = 500 mL

WEIGHTS (mass)

½ ounce = 15 g
1 ounce = 30 g
3 ounces = 90 g
4 ounces = 120 g
8 ounces = 225 g
10 ounces = 285 g
12 ounces = 360 g
16 ounces = 1 pound = 450 g

DIMENSIONS

1/16 inch = 2 mm
⅛ inch = 3 mm
¼ inch = 6 mm
½ inch = 1.5 cm
¾ inch = 2 cm
1 inch = 2.5 cm

OVEN TEMPERATURES

250°F = 120°C
275°F = 140°C
300°F = 150°C
325°F = 160°C
350°F = 180°C
375°F = 190°C
400°F = 200°C
425°F = 220°C
450°F = 230°C

BAKING PAN SIZES

Utensil	Size in Inches/Quarts	Metric Volume	Size in Centimeters
Baking or	8×8×2	2 L	20×20×5
Cake Pan	9×9×2	2.5 L	22×22×5
(square or	12×8×2	3 L	30×20×5
rectangular)	13×9×2	3.5 L	33×23×5
Loaf Pan	8×4×3	1.5 L	20×10×7
	9×5×3	2 L	23×13×7
Round Layer	8×1½	1.2 L	20×4
Cake Pan	9×1½	1.5 L	23×4
Pie Plate	8×1¼	750 mL	20×3
	9×1¼	1 L	23×3
Baking Dish	1 quart	1 L	—
or Casserole	1½ quart	1.5 L	—
	2 quart	2 L	—